Contents

Introduction

Develop your emotional intelligence (EQ) to stand out in the fast-paced and complex professional world. Enhance your awareness of emotions and triggers, and manage your responses positively. Cultivate social awareness to build strong relationships. Unlike fixed traits, emotional intelligence can be developed over time, offering opportunities for personal and professional growth. Focus on the four quadrants: self-awareness, self-management, social awareness, and relationship management. Learn and practice these skills to connect meaningfully with others, navigate challenges, and achieve desired results in your career.

Successful companies are not successful by chance; they have exceptional teams, execute well, and benefit from some luck. However, at the core of every great company is a well-crafted strategy. The term "strategy" may have various interpretations, but, for me, it is about assessing all available opportunities and choosing the most fitting one for our organization. It begins by answering the question: Amid all our potential actions, where should we focus our time and attention? It is akin to standing at the foot of a mountain range, surveying the peaks, and determining which one, uniquely suited to us, we will pursue.

Creating a team where everyone feels heard and understood is a common desire, particularly in the current landscape of hybrid and remote work. We will learn the importance of empathy, compassion, and authentic listening in communication for effective leadership. We will cover both the mindset and skillset of communication to enhance team engagement, productivity, and motivation. We will understand how to lead with compassion and curiosity while fostering a culture of psychological safety.

We will reshape our perception of trust, a complex and crucial concept in our lives. Trust, often casually used, plays a vital role in navigating risk, managing uncertainty, embracing vulnerability, and having faith in the unknown. Comparing trust to money provides a useful analogy. While money is tangible, trust is a subjective human feeling, making it challenging to measure or define universally. I strive to offer a precise language and a clear framework to transform your understanding of trust, highlighting its fragility and immense value in both personal and professional realms.

Navigating challenges like firing someone, delivering tough feedback, or managing employees' emotions can be demanding for a manager. We will explore quick scripts for nine challenging topics to help you handle tough conversations with confidence and ease. While these situations may not be enjoyable, having these scripts can serve as a valuable starting point in your role as a manager.

If your team is facing uncertainty, shift your focus from protecting them to empowering them. Create a stable work environment that restores their energy and gives them control over significant outcomes. This empowerment will enable them to take meaningful actions to navigate change and disruption successfully.

As a leader, you encounter diverse personalities daily. To be effective, you must master the skills of motivating, leading, and persuading individuals. We will explore the essential skills to lead and motivate every team member successfully.

We often experience challenges of juggling multiple responsibilities, especially in these stressful times. The good news is that with intention, you can become a more human leader. Focus on four key aspects: communication for connections, a reconsideration of all meetings, making professional development a collective effort, and fostering a culture of well-being.

Addressing mental health at work is an essential and non-negotiable discussion. It goes beyond wellness and is integral to professional development. We will provide insights into approaching this conversation from a leadership perspective, defining your role, and offering specific strategies for initiating, receiving, and managing these discussions as a manager.

Chapter 1 Developing Your Emotional Intelligence

Managing your mindset

As you read this book, your brain processes various stimuli—background noise, physical sensations, and internal thoughts. To manage this information overload, your brain relies on cognitive shortcuts. However, these shortcuts can sometimes lead to negative emotional triggers, causing unhelpful interpretations and responses to situations. Triggers may relate to specific situations or individuals, generating recurring emotions and thoughts. Reflect on challenges from the past six months, identify recurring themes, and analyze how emotions impact your responses. Recognizing triggers enhances self-awareness and empowers you to respond more effectively.

Finding your flow

To enhance your emotional intelligence, focus on engaging in activities that bring you satisfaction and joy, creating a state of flow. Flow, a concept from positive psychology, involves participating in challenging, enjoyable activities that captivate your concentration and stretch your abilities. This state not only boosts performance and skill development but also provides a positive emotional experience, fostering engagement, interest, and a sense of achievement. Identifying your flow activities and incorporating them into your work can strengthen psychological resilience, positively influencing how you approach challenges and reinforcing the belief in your ability to tackle them effectively.

Disrupting thoughts and emotional intelligence

Disrupting the impact of emotions on your thoughts and behavior can be achieved using the ABCDE model from cognitive behavioral coaching. A: Identify the activating event objectively, avoiding subjective judgments. B: Explore your beliefs and thoughts about the event, including emotional responses. C: Assess the consequences of your beliefs on emotions and behavior. D: Introduce disrupting thoughts to replace unhelpful beliefs. E: Evaluate the effects of challenging your thoughts on emotional responses and outcomes. Apply this model to situations, like an unproductive conversation, to gain a clearer perspective, manage emotions, and improve reactions. Regularly practicing this exercise helps identify emotional triggers and enhances emotional resilience in challenging work situations.

Dealing with stressful situations

Acting on emotional impulses can yield positive or negative outcomes depending on the emotions involved. To break the quick chain between thought, emotion, and response, practice slowing down your reaction time. Step one: Identify emotional reactions when objectivity is needed. Step two: Take a step back and create space when feeling strong emotions like anger or fear. Step three: Allow time for recovery before making decisions. Choose how to respond thoughtfully, enhancing the likelihood of positive outcomes. Developing this habit requires practice, especially in situations where emotions run high. Creating space, regulating physiological symptoms, and consciously choosing responses contribute to better outcomes.

Shift perspective to shape behavior

Cultivating the ability to see things from different perspectives is advantageous, especially when passionate about a topic. Actively seek alternative opinions and arguments, viewing them as opportunities for learning and innovation. Asking more questions, listening actively, and spending time with diverse individuals contribute to broadening perspectives and building relationships. Reading regularly, even in short intervals, aids in exploring various viewpoints. Reflect on past experiences when considering multiple angles led to effective responses, emphasizing the importance of a well-developed perspective.

Developing social awareness

Enhancing emotional intelligence involves developing both self-awareness and social awareness. To cultivate social awareness, focus on your senses—observe, listen, and feel in various situations. Conduct a sensory audit by dedicating 20 minutes to keenly observe your surroundings. Practice using your senses to gather information about others, interpreting facial expressions, body language, and tone of voice. Paying attention to these details helps you understand people's thoughts and dynamics between them. Strengthen your ability to notice these cues amid life's demands, allowing you to engage more effectively with others.

Looking past empathy: Connecting with perspective

Understanding perspectives is crucial, especially for those who find empathizing challenging. Instead of solely focusing on empathy, concentrate on grasping diverse viewpoints. This involves acknowledging and respecting others' views without necessarily sharing their emotions. Reflect on people's experiences and consider various possibilities without assuming exact feelings. Before meetings, set the intention to learn about others' perspectives, and actively explore their viewpoints during interactions. Asking questions like, "Tell me more about where you are coming from" fosters understanding, simplifies negotiations, and builds strong relationships, contributing to effective communication in challenging situations.

Listen to improve social awareness

Effective communication involves not only expressing your point but also actively listening to others. Listening to their words, tone, and body language is crucial for building strong relationships and finding collaborative solutions. While emotions may drive the desire to speak, taking a step back, pausing, and truly understanding others' viewpoints enhance effective communication. Reflect on your listening skills and identify opportunities for improvement. Set intentions to learn during interactions, challenging yourself to discover at least one new thing in each exchange. After meetings, note down what you learned, fostering a habit of active listening for balanced information flow in communication.

Authentic adaptability

Authentic communication builds trust over time. While adapting to different situations is essential, understanding your natural communication strengths is crucial. Identify your strengths, such as clarity, active listening, creating a comfortable atmosphere, or connecting authentically. Ask trusted individuals for feedback on your strengths. Be adaptable in your communication style, adjusting tone and energy level without compromising authenticity. Match your communication style to the other person, considering factors like energy level and preferences. Stay true to your values while being mindful of effective communication. Reflect on the other person's style before conversations and adjust your approach to foster productive dialogue.

EQ and positive conflict management

Conflicts at work, when managed positively, foster creativity and productivity. Utilizing emotional intelligence in conflict resolution is crucial. Establish team rules for engagement, defining healthy debate and addressing challenges collaboratively. Respectful disagreement strengthens relationships and builds trust over time. Practice "plus" by adding constructive suggestions when challenging ideas, promoting a thoughtful and constructive culture. Avoid using oppositional phrases like "Yes, but" and opt for alternatives like "Yes, and" or "What if" to enhance communication. Embrace conflict as a tool for continuous improvement, aiming for a workplace where disagreements contribute to solid connections and relationships, supported by emotional intelligence.

Communicate intention and impact

Be mindful that how you intend to come across may differ from how others perceive you. Adaptability in communication is crucial, focusing on the intention behind your message rather than the exact words. For instance, a sales manager can tailor communication based on individual preferences, whether through one-to-one briefings, emails, or casual conversations. Emphasize your intent before interactions to enhance focus and flexibility. Understanding your intentions builds trust, boosts confidence, and allows for authenticity. Recognize that effective communication is about the message received, not just the one delivered. Before meetings, clarify your intent to guide the interaction's direction or the desired emotional outcome.

EQ development plan

Creating lasting change in your life involves more than just understanding emotional intelligence; it requires action through a development plan. Start by envisioning your goals—consider strong team relationships or heightened self-awareness. Define your mission, exploring the personal reasons behind your pursuit. Establish clear goals, such as regular meetings or daily journaling, and outline specific tactics to achieve them. Lastly, establish measures to track your progress. This strategic approach empowers you to shape your future, achieving both professional and personal milestones.

Chapter 2 How to Think Strategically

First rule of strategy

To identify the right opportunity, focus on solving significant challenges uniquely suited to your capabilities. Great companies like Amazon, Disney, and Nike excel by addressing substantial problems with no substitutes in the eyes of their customers. The key to profitable strategy lies in capturing a substantial portion of the value you create. If your solution is unique, you can charge more and capture a larger share. However, if your solution has substitutes, profits diminish. The ability to deliver exceptional, irreplaceable value is the hallmark of a successful business.

Sizing the mountain

Identifying the right opportunity involves choosing a significant challenge that aligns with your unique capabilities. To assess the size of this challenge, consider factors such as the current market size, growth rate, and latent demand. Market size reflects current spending on the challenge, while growth rate indicates trends. Latent demand represents unsolved problems in the market. For instance, Apple's potential entry into the luxury car market illustrates the concept of envisioning a market's potential beyond its current state. Startups often focus on addressing latent demand to expand markets. When evaluating a problem and sizing a market, analyze current size, growth trajectory, and latent demand to determine how you can contribute and potentially grow the market. This process aligns with the idea of the basis of competition, guiding your ascent to the top.

Basis of competition and capabilities

After sizing our mountain, the next step is understanding the terrain, which involves identifying what customers value and distinguishes companies in terms of loyalty. This relates to the basis of competition, where factors like product durability, ease of use, and integration matter to customers. Each market has its basis of competition—factors influencing customers to choose one company over others. Successful companies deeply understand the problem they're solving and, by doing so, earn the right to address it for the world. Amazon is a notable example, starting as an e-commerce site for book enthusiasts and later expanding its basis of competition to factors like selection, customer confidence, and speedy delivery. The second rule of strategy emphasizes strategic alignment achieved through a clear understanding of the problem, defining the basis of competition, and building capabilities that uniquely serve customers.

The benefits of scale

After choosing our mountain, sizing it up, understanding the basis of competition, and planning unique capabilities, it is crucial to recognize the role of scale in market effectiveness. Profits and value predominantly favor market leaders, but the significance of scale varies across industries. Consider a chart where effectiveness increases with height, representing customer satisfaction, while business size expands from left to right. In the restaurant industry, adding more locations has modest benefits. Semiconductors, with high entry costs, demonstrate the importance of reaching a substantial scale to be effective. Ride-sharing, exemplified by Uber, initially struggles with few drivers but plateaus in value beyond a certain point. Each industry's scale dynamics differ, emphasizing the need to understand your business's curve and operate accordingly. Scale advantages stem from cost scale (economies in production), innovation scale (more benefits from problem-solving), and network effects (increased product value with growth). It is essential to comprehend how scale operates in your industry to establish effective strategies and achieve market leadership.

Disruption

After achieving scale, companies can still lose their way, as demonstrated by shifts in market leaders over time. It is vital to recognize patterns of successful companies losing their market position. Returning to the original framework of choosing a mountain, understanding the basis of competition, and developing necessary capabilities, any change in these dynamics can render a strategy obsolete.

Consider the mountain as market leadership, with different terrains to reach the top. Changes can occur in the size of the mountain when problems become obsolete, like the shift from film to digital photography. The basis of competition can change, as seen in the shift to electric vehicles in the automobile industry. Additionally, advancements in capabilities, such as new technologies, can alter effectiveness.

For instance, Howard Head revolutionized ski design by applying aeronautical engineering, rendering traditional wooden skis obsolete. Consumer behavior changes, known as disruption, often involve substitutes that are lower cost or easier to use, like mobile phones replacing digital cameras.

Market evolution can also lead to the realization that your mountaintop is a foothill in a larger mountain range. In software, the focus shifted from specific solutions to integrated products that serve a range of use cases. This shift is similar to the concept of scope, understanding the full periphery of the problem to win in the marketplace.

Conversely, unbundling occurs when a company identifies a crucial subset of a larger problem that the market leader does not serve well. Instagram, focusing on photo sharing, is an example, ultimately prompting Facebook's acquisition.

To avoid losing their way, companies must assess whether the size of the mountain, the basis of competition, or the required capabilities have changed. Adapting strategies to evolving dynamics ensures continued success.

Business model architecture

An often overlooked but crucial aspect of strategy is business model architecture, ensuring that how you charge for products aligns your interests with your customers. This alignment is vital in the pursuit of creating incremental value for both parties. Many successful tech companies, among the world's most valuable, adopt models like subscriptions, aligning their interests closely with customers. Contrasting this with traditional technology sales, where licenses were sold, the alignment of interests was lacking. In subscription models, the goal is to renew contracts annually, emphasizing effective communication of value and continuous improvement to build enduring customer relationships. When the commercial model aligns with customer value, it contributes to the success of an exceptional business.

Value creation patterns

Like any art form, inspiration for effective strategies can be drawn from diverse sources. Consider industries you may not have thought of before but share similarities with yours. Take, for instance, the parallels between movie companies and pharmaceuticals. Movie companies seek blockbusters by carefully selecting ideas through stages of production, aiming for quick scaling and distribution. Similarly, pharmaceutical companies face comparable challenges in bringing unique therapeutics to market. By examining these patterns of discovery, execution, and distribution across different industries, you can glean insights to enhance your effectiveness in conquering your strategic challenges.

Next steps

To conclude on a personal note, I believe great strategies revolve around three key concepts: solving unique problems for people, adapting to changes for ongoing leadership, and fostering a business where your success aligns with your customers'. These principles not only define a great strategy but also contribute to a fulfilling career.

Chapter 3 Communication Skills for Modern Management

The evolution of communication

Communication has evolved significantly with advancing technologies, especially in the context of the pandemic, leading to a shift in how we connect and interact. The new work environment requires managers to go beyond task-oriented communication and prioritize the well-being of individuals. This involves transitioning from transactional to compassionate communication and from a command-and-control approach to one of curiosity and collaboration. While technology is crucial, it cannot replace the need for empathy, compassion, and a sense of belonging. We will focus on expanding both mindset and skillset, emphasizing non-judgmental listening and compassionate understanding. It provides tools for fostering open and healthy dialogue in remote work scenarios, ensuring employees feel heard, valued, and collaborative efforts result in innovative solutions. As communication remains an essential managerial skill, adapting to these changes is vital.

A communication framework for the modern workplace

Evaluate your communication's impact by considering whether it fosters dialogue or shuts it down. Establishing a robust communication foundation is crucial, focusing on three key factors: Trust, Honesty, and Empathy (T.H.E.). Assess your trustworthiness on a scale of 1 to 10, reflecting on your consistency in keeping promises and creating a safe environment for open communication. Honesty, the second factor, involves transparency and delivering feedback respectfully. Rate your honesty on a similar scale and identify areas for improvement. Lastly, empathy, the third factor, is vital for creating a supportive environment where team members feel seen and understood. Rate your empathy and pinpoint potential variations among team members. Strengthen your communication foundation by addressing the factor with the lowest rating.

This will enhance your overall communication impact and contribute to stronger relationships and goal achievement.

Communication plus listening equal impact

Effective communication involves not only directed communication but also attentive listening. While delivering information and presenting are crucial, great managers excel in listening, fostering an inclusive and productive environment. A McKinsey study highlights the correlation between feeling included in workplace communication and increased productivity. Mastering both directed communication and listening is essential for impactful communication. Reflect on your listening habits by assessing how often you make assumptions, explain more than listen, think ahead of the speaker, or let emotions interfere. Identify areas for improvement, and commit to enhancing your listening skills. Self-awareness is key, especially in remote work settings where body language cues are limited. By making small changes and staying curious during conversations, you can create a space where others feel heard and understood, ultimately improving overall communication.

The three biggest barriers to effective communication

The initial step towards enhancing communication is self-awareness, a challenging yet invaluable gift. Unwrapping this gift involves a critical examination of how we communicate, respond, and react, and the hindrances to effectiveness. Three major barriers—your mind (assumptions, judgments, and beliefs about others), your emotions (especially in high-stress situations), and your environment (constraints like time, money, and resources)—impact day-to-day interactions. Reflect on which barrier predominantly affects your interactions and note it down. As you engage with your team, be mindful of these barriers, observe their occurrence, and consider their impact, laying the foundation for later tools to overcome them.

The top quality of a great communicator

Think about recent conversations where you may have felt disconnected or distracted by internal thoughts. Often, we unknowingly engage in a dialogue with our inner critic, hindering effective communication. Curiosity, characterized by genuine interest and openness, is a vital skill for great communicators. Curiosity and judgment cannot coexist simultaneously. An experiment involving judgment and curiosity demonstrates this. To foster curiosity, set aside internal distractions, release judgments, and accept others without necessarily agreeing with them. Cultivating curiosity opens your heart and mind, making you more receptive and fostering effective communication. Practice using the simple question, "I wonder," to encourage curiosity. Shift your focus from yourself to others in your conversations this week, fostering stronger relationships and deeper trust. Embrace curiosity to become the adaptive manager the current times demand.

Be clear about expectations

Nearly every team issue can be traced back to communication breakdowns—miscommunication, misunderstandings, or lack of communication. To mitigate this, it is crucial to establish clear expectations with your team consistently and early, especially in a remote work setting where actions can be easily misinterpreted. Identify recurring issues in your projects, like personality clashes, missed deadlines, or scope changes, and proactively discuss how to address them as a team before they occur. Engage in team-norming sessions using a table of questions to set expectations, creating communication norms around key issues. Addressing expectations upfront helps teams navigate challenges more efficiently and provides a structured way for individuals uncomfortable with conflict to communicate gracefully. This proactive approach minimizes finger-pointing and fosters a culture where team members expect and appreciate ongoing discussions about expectations. Setting clear expectations, both for addressing common issues and defining team roles, is vital for effective management and project success. Regularly revisit and update expectations based on evolving team dynamics and project needs to ensure ongoing clarity and productivity.

Ask questions to motivate and inspire

Fostering a sense of belonging and open communication within your team is essential. The pandemic highlighted the importance of honest and healthy communication, emphasizing the need for environments where team members feel heard and understood. Curiosity plays a key role in effective communication, with powerful questions being a tool used by great communicators. Powerful questions typically start with "what" or "how," opening up dialogue and avoiding defensive responses often triggered by "why" questions. Compassion questions like "Can you help me understand?" facilitate open conversations. Shifting from directive statements to curious inquiries, especially during one conversation a day, can transform team communication and create a culture of engagement, where team members feel valued and heard.

Listen so others feel heard, valued, and understood

Effective listening involves multiple layers that significantly impact communication. The first layer, the "me" layer, occurs when our attention is self-centered, leading to disengagement. Shifting to the second layer, "you," involves being curious and focusing on the other person, recognizing body language, and addressing unspoken concerns. The "play dumb" technique helps explore intuitive feelings, fostering open dialogue. Moving beyond individual interactions, the third layer involves team dynamics, especially in remote meetings. By practicing curiosity and the play dumb technique, you can enhance your listening skills and identify the layer you're in, promoting more meaningful communication.

The power of the pause

Effective communication involves not only what we say but also the power of silence. We will explore the impact of pauses in conversations. Pausing creates a space for authentic contributions from others. Recognizing the challenge of pausing, especially for fast communicators, is essential. Recording meetings or calls can help assess your communication pace. Practice pausing after sharing your perspective or asking a question. Count to three internally, allowing others to contribute. Embrace the discomfort, use humor to address silence, and open up dialogues. Incorporating pauses in communication fosters meaningful interactions and becomes more natural with practice.

Communicate responsibly

Managers play a crucial role in shaping the impact of their communication. Recognizing the types of communication is vital: reckless communication involves gossiping, negativity, and interruptions; responsible communication entails giving direct feedback, focusing on solutions, and taking accountability; silent communication involves going mute for various reasons. Instead of staying silent, adopting responsible communication by expressing the need for time or assistance, acknowledging lack of knowledge, or specifying a busy schedule is crucial. Evaluate recent interactions, identify areas of improvement, and strive to positively impact conversations. Responsible communication fosters psychological safety and serves as a role model for others.

Say this not that

The language we use can significantly influence communication, relationships, and team dynamics. Instead of asking, "Is this clear?" or "Do you understand?" which often leads to misunderstandings, encourage others to paraphrase what they've understood. Starting sentences with unnecessary phrases like "To be honest" or "Actually" diminishes the impact of your message; it's more effective to state your point directly. Avoid starting sentences with directives like "Look" or "Listen," as they can be perceived as imposing. Eliminate pre-apologizing before stating a point to appear more confident. Minimize the use of "just" in your vocabulary, as it can weaken communication. Replace "but" with "and" to create a more positive and impactful message. Identify which words or phrases you currently use and commit to practicing a shift for more powerful and confident communication.

How to say "no" and set boundaries with grace

A common communication challenge is gracefully saying no and setting boundaries, especially for those who tend to say yes to please others. To effectively navigate this, first, clarify your priorities. Then, take time to prepare your response, acknowledging and naming any emotions involved. Script out your response using a guideline provided, which involves acknowledging the situation, empathizing, and stating possibilities or limitations. Finally, make a request or suggestion for a solution. Practice this three-step process when needed, whether in-person or remotely. Mastering the art of setting boundaries empowers you and sets an example for others.

Conversation closers

After productive one-on-one or team meetings, it is crucial to close with clear actions and deadlines to avoid later issues. Use the "Three Closer Questions" to reinforce accountability:

1. What will you take on and by when?

2. How do you want to be held accountable?

3. If something comes up, what should I expect?

These questions empower team members to state their actions, choose their preferred accountability method, and address potential issues in advance. By giving them ownership, you foster commitment and minimize the need for micromanagement.

Communicating across the globe

It is crucial to recognize that these tools are not universally applicable; effective communication varies based on individual preferences and cultural differences. To navigate such differences, it's essential to inquire about preferences and cultural expectations in advance. Regardless of the duration of your collaboration, asking these questions remains pertinent, especially in virtual work settings. By proactively understanding etiquette, you enhance your communication skills and adaptability, contributing to more effective collaboration. As you prepare for future one-on-one meetings, consider reviewing insights into preferred communication styles and improve your effectiveness.

Communicating during one-on-one meetings

How well do you understand your team members? The level of personal knowledge about each team member can vary among managers, ranging from a focus on professional matters to those who delve into personal aspects. The pandemic provided a unique opportunity to glimpse into people's lives, fostering vulnerability and empathy. While team meetings are crucial for alignment, the one-on-one meeting offers a chance to connect deeply and understand team members. The frequency and purpose of these meetings should be discussed to maximize their value. Successful one-on-ones hinge on creating an open environment and asking powerful questions that allow team members to share their needs and concerns. Questions like "What do you need from me to ensure your success?" and "What can I do differently that might be hindering your success?" can offer valuable insights. Additionally, questions about their gifts, talents, and motivations contribute to a deeper understanding. Spread these questions over time, give them in advance, and encourage thoughtful responses for more effective conversations. In essence, genuinely caring about and understanding your team members fosters a positive environment where they feel valued, heard, and motivated to perform at their best.

Be a super communicator

We have explored essential aspects of modern managerial communication, from foundational principles to specific tools. The modern manager excels in asking insightful questions, recognizing the whole individual, practicing compassionate listening, and leading with curiosity and collaboration. This includes valuing emotional intelligence, maintaining a growth mindset, and fostering psychological safety. While the mindset and skills covered serve as an initial step, ongoing learning is crucial. Success is measured by applying these skills and mindset to daily interactions. It is time to translate learning into action and become the modern manager demanded by contemporary workplaces.

Chapter 4 Why Trust Matters

The real meaning of trust

Consider someone in your life whom you deeply trust—someone dependable, whether it's a family member, partner, friend, or colleague. Now, think about someone who places immense trust in you and reflect on how they perceive that trust. While people can describe the feelings associated with trust, defining it is challenging. Trust has more definitions than even love and happiness. Exploring visual representations of trust, such as someone jumping over a gap or a lion with a mouse, reveals a common thread: a blend of vulnerability and expectations. These fusion forms the essence of trust. From this perspective, trust is a confident relationship with the unknown. This definition unveils how trust empowers us to navigate uncertainty, have faith in strangers, and confront the unknown. The level of trust required increases with the degree of uncertainty and the unknown.

Challenging assumptions about trust

There are three misconceptions about trust. First, it is not always about having more trust; the goal is to give our trust to those who are trustworthy. Second, the notion of "building trust" is misleading; instead, trust is continuously earned, not something you construct. Finally, avoid the idea of blanket trust; trust is contextual and subjective, involving trusting someone to perform specific actions.

The psychology of risk

Consider a moment in your life when you embraced change or took a significant risk, such as using a self-driving car or engaging in cryptocurrency. Risk, defined as exposure to uncertainty with potential loss, operates as a formula: risk equals likelihood times severity. Trust and risk are intertwined, with trust serving as the force that enables us to navigate the bridge from the known to the unknown. This dynamic is visualized as a "trust leap," representing instances when we take risks to explore new or fundamentally different actions. Recognizing this relationship underscores the vital role of trust in fostering innovation and facilitating the journey of new ideas.

How to take a trust leap

As a child, we were often cautioned not to trust strangers, yet today, we willingly enter cars with strangers through services like Uber and stay in people's homes globally. Understanding why trust leaps, once considered risky, have become commonplace behaviors for many requires examining the barriers that impede such leaps. Three key barriers are social proof, which involves showcasing that others have successfully taken the leap; loss aversion, acknowledging people's fear of loss more than the pleasure of gain; and the law of familiarity, emphasizing the importance of the familiar done differently. Addressing these barriers is crucial in facilitating the transition from the known, where people feel in control and safe, to the unknown. Focusing solely on the novelty and benefits of a trust leap without addressing underlying fears may overlook fundamental human tendencies.

What to do when trust breaks down

Distrust is not simply the opposite of trust; it is distinct from low trust or a lack of trust. Low trust may be akin to ambivalence or uncertainty, while distrust involves fiery emotions such as blame, defensiveness, and aggression. Distrust arises from a confident belief that the other person's intent is to cause harm, tapping into our vulnerability and fear. Once mistrust transforms into distrust, recovery becomes challenging, whether in personal relationships or within companies facing a trust crisis. When distrust sets in, the instinctive human response is to flee, be defensive, or turn away as a protective mechanism to ensure safety.

Busting the myth of trust and transparency

The common notion that increased transparency leads to more trust is flawed. While transparency is often seen as a remedy for trust issues, it does not necessarily enhance trust. In reality, transparency can reduce the need for trust, as seen in various situations where individuals seek more information or surveillance due to declining trust. The misconception stems from the belief that secrets and secrecy are trust's enemies, but the real adversary is deception. Transparency alone is not a solution to address deception and foster trust.

The relationship between trust and vulnerability

When trust transforms into distrust, it signifies a loss of the currency that facilitates interaction. Companies facing a trust crisis may still make money but lose the permission to engage with individuals in the same way. Distrust can be mutual, leading to a breakdown in interaction. To move on from trust issues, it's crucial to believe in cultural and structural changes that prevent a recurrence. Addressing trust issues promptly is vital, as lingering distrust can spread rapidly. Recovery from distrust often involves an honest and vulnerable conversation, creating a powerful loop of vulnerability that contributes to rebuilding trust. This delicate balance between knowing when to be vulnerable and the reciprocal act of catching vulnerability is crucial for fostering trust. In high-trust cultures, the continuous presence of this Vulnerability Loop is a defining feature.

Deciding if someone is trustworthy: Capability

One of the crucial aspects of trust is determining whom to trust and what makes someone trustworthy. The science behind trust reveals four traits, divided into capability traits and character traits. Capability traits consist of competence and reliability. Competence involves assessing whether a person possesses the skills, resources, and knowledge needed for a task, while reliability focuses on respecting time and maintaining consistent behavior over time. It is important to note that confidence does not always equate to competence, and capability is highly contextual. These capability traits address how someone accomplishes tasks.

Deciding if someone is trustworthy: Character

To determine someone's trustworthiness, it is crucial to assess their character traits, focusing on integrity and empathy. People often rely on intuition or gut feelings, but there are concrete questions and signals to evaluate these traits. Empathy involves being conscious of how one's actions impact others and the ability to tolerate differing beliefs. Integrity, the most important trait, centers on honesty, intentions, and motives. Trust breakdowns often stem from character issues rather than capability problems. Understanding and applying these traits can lead to smarter decision-making and evaluating trustworthiness in various aspects of life.

The power of trust

Being human entails trust, an essential element in our daily activities. With a precise understanding of trust—what it is, how it functions, and its significance—we gain control over it. We determine whom we trust, assess our own trustworthiness, and make decisions about taking risks or holding back. Trust serves as a powerful force, a social glue that empowers us to navigate uncertainty and change effectively.

Chapter 5 Quick Scripts for Difficult Conversations

Script to terminate someone

Terminating an employee is often the most difficult task for many managers. People often feel uneasy and struggle to find the right words—either saying too little or too much. Having a well-prepared talk track is crucial. Here is a script example: "Johnny, I regret to inform you that I am terminating your employment, effective today. Despite our discussions about the necessary improvements in your work, I have not observed the changes we discussed. I have consistently asked for proactive project updates and clear communication of team goals to no avail. As a result, I have decided to make a change." Following this, address the logistical details, such as the last day, severance, and insurance. Be prepared for questions, and conclude the conversation by expressing gratitude for their contributions and wishing them well. Firing someone is undoubtedly challenging, but using a script can provide the confidence and guidance needed in this tough managerial task.

Script of the conversation before you terminate someone

Before terminating someone, it is crucial to have a clear, direct conversation outlining concerns and expectations. Here is a pre-termination script:

"Samantha, we need to have a serious conversation. I have given you feedback, and I want absolute clarity on my concerns and the changes required. Key metrics have been consistently down, and I need to see improvement. Work with your team to address this without causing stress or burnout. You must be more responsive to peers and set clear expectations. I am willing to brainstorm solutions and support you, but you must take full ownership and show improvement in the next two months. Failure to do so will lead to our next discussion being about your departure from the business. Let's discuss this further, and I'm here to assist. Be direct, maintain a neutral tone, and be prepared to address questions, ensuring your message is clear and leaves no room for ambiguity."

Script to lay someone off with compassion

Laying someone off is a challenging task that requires clarity and compassion. When delivering the news, start by expressing appreciation for their professional contributions. Clearly state that the job is being eliminated due to necessary cuts for the company's sustainability. Provide details about the situation, such as the percentage of cuts and assure them it is not performance-related. Express gratitude for their contributions and offer support in their job search. Discuss severance and health insurance details and allow time for processing. If available, involve an HR partner in the conversation for additional support. Maintain a compassionate yet clear tone, avoiding negative comments about the company's decisions. The focus should be on facts and reassurance of their fair treatment.

Script for positive feedback

Long ago, during a manager training session, a participant shared a preference for negative feedback, finding it more helpful than positive feedback. Many struggles with giving effective positive feedback, so having scripts can be useful. Here are a few examples:

1. "Hey Molly, great job on cleaning up the data in our system. Your high-level strategy combined with hard work was seamless and cheerful. I appreciate your organization, collaboration with colleagues, and keeping me updated."

2. "Hey Tony, despite delays on your project, I see your hard work and calm crisis management. Your ownership and team focus are commendable. Keep it up, and you'll reach the finish line."

3. "Nancy, I've noticed you've been quiet in meetings. Just wanted to check in and see how you're doing. My door is always open for anything you want to talk about."

These scripts convey appreciation, show that you notice and care about your employees, and help them recognize their efforts.

Script for direct, diplomatic, difficult feedback

When leaders complain about their employees, I often ask if they have communicated the issues. Typically, the response is a delayed plan for the next performance review or vague gestures. Providing constructive feedback is challenging but essential. Make it easier with these scripts. Begin by clarifying the goal—to change behavior, not vent frustration. Maintain a controlled tone and start by asking if it's a good time to discuss. For example, "I've noticed project delays without communication, impacting the team. Let's work on realistic deadlines and proactive communication. Can you see my point?" Facilitate discussion, offer assistance, and end with clear next steps. Your role is to support their success through direct and diplomatic feedback.

Script to hold someone accountable

When discussing accountability with leaders, the focus is not on firing employees for minor issues but on fostering clear conversations to enhance ownership. Maintaining a tone that's more curious than furious is crucial. Use this script: "I've observed a decline in overall team productivity and heard concerns about team dynamics. Let's discuss and plan improvements together. I'm here to support, emphasizing team ownership. What are your thoughts and proposed actions?" Ensure a follow-up to track progress and reinforce the importance of accountability. Consistency in this structure will help maintain clarity.

Script to tell someone they'll have a new boss

In corporate America, a practice known as layering involves placing a new manager above an existing employee who then reports to the new manager. While this is often done to support departmental growth, the employee being layered may perceive it as a demotion. To address this, use the following script: "Glen, I'm bringing in a new leader for our department, and you'll report to them. Your leadership has been crucial, and now, as we face new challenges, we need someone with specific experience. This person will support your skill development, enabling you to grow into a larger role. I value your thoughts on this and any questions you have. Let's discuss how you feel about this change and address your concerns." Remember to show compassion and have a heart-to-heart discussion about their development needs, helping them formulate a proactive development plan. This approach emphasizes growth opportunities during a period of change.

Script for when an employee cries or gets defensive

You're striving to be an effective manager, providing timely feedback and fostering employee growth. However, when faced with defensive or teary reactions, it can be challenging. Anticipate emotional responses, stay composed, and address the situation constructively. If someone gets defensive, acknowledge their feelings, express your intention to have a constructive conversation, and inquire about their perspective. Then, discuss ways to ensure future conversations remain constructive. If the individual is upset, consider suggesting a temporary pause and returning to the discussion later. When someone gets teary, express empathy, offer a moment if needed, and propose resuming the conversation at a more suitable time. Managing emotions is part of the managerial role, and these scripts aim to help navigate such situations gracefully.

Script for when someone didn't get the promotion

If an employee pursues a promotion and does not succeed, it is crucial to handle the conversation delicately. Communicate the news empathetically, acknowledging their strengths and accomplishments. Highlight the specific qualifications needed for the role and express confidence in their future. Offer to discuss their career path and create a development plan in the coming weeks to keep them motivated and engaged despite the setback.

Chapter 6 Leading with Stability during Times of Change and Disruption

Creating stability amidst disruption

Change can be unsettling due to the brain's predictive nature. Discomfort arises as the brain's fight or flight response kicks in to restore predictability. Neuroscientist David Eagleman highlights the importance of staying open to novel experiences, which can enhance the brain's adaptability. Teams in uncertain environments either thrive or struggle, largely influenced by the leaders' focus on building stability. To create stability for your team, start by managing the initial impact of disruption, co-create stability with the team, empower them to proactively counterbalance disruption, and coach them to build confidence amid ongoing changes. This approach not only fosters stability but also cultivates agility, a crucial skill for the future workplace.

Demonstrate empathy

In times of disruption, the key is to ensure that individuals feel heard, understood, and witnessed, which embodies empathy. Drawing on the example of the 2019 pandemic, where cognitive load was overwhelming, human-to-human support grounded people in survival mode. Demonstrating empathy, particularly through active listening, is crucial for teams navigating change. To achieve active listening, resist immediately moving into solution mode, use cues like nodding and affirming sounds, play back what's been shared, and ask powerful, open-ended questions. Michael Bungay Stanier's "And what else?" technique can elevate empathy, uncovering valuable insights.

Focus on well-being

Well-being is a personalized concept, but a universal aspect is recognizing the importance of rest in maintaining resilience. Trust is essential when it comes to taking rest – trust in one's instincts, colleagues, and future self. In the face of change or a toxic culture, constant alertness makes switching off challenging. To foster a healthy approach to rest across your team, prioritize psychological safety by modeling openness about boundaries and low moments. Develop a well-being rescue plan, a team agreement for supporting downtime, and encourage resilience accountability partners to advise on setting boundaries and suggest breaks when needed. Recognize that while work is beneficial, pushing beyond limits can lead to burnout, emphasizing the need for a supportive environment during disruptions.

Empower your team

You cannot shield your team from uncertainty, but instead of dwelling on external factors beyond their control, redirect their focus to experiences they can influence. Psychologist Julian B. Rotter's concept of Locus of Control, established in 1954, underscores the positive outcomes linked to the belief in one's ability to affect change. In the workplace, having control over workload, work location, and team dynamics correlates with enhanced performance, increased well-being, and engagement. Concentrating on manageable aspects buffers stress from uncontrollable disruptions. After addressing the initial disruption, guide your team to concentrate on the right things within their control—such as team vision, clarity, and optimizing work routines. This empowers them to protect themselves from discomfort caused by uncontrollable factors, fostering a belief in their agency and building long-term resilience.

Cocreate a vision

A clear vision aids in creating certainty, shifting focus from disruption-related uncertainty to meaningful changes. It also helps identify opportunities, as setting specific goals activates the brain's planning center, honing in on progress. Additionally, a shared vision fosters team connection, aligning efforts toward a collective goal. To create a vision, focus on making it aspirational, meaningful, and inclusive. Do not obsess over perfection; the vision can evolve. Conduct inclusive sessions to discuss and finalize the vision, fostering team stability, effective leadership, and future-oriented focus.

Rethink your routine

Routine brings predictability, stability, and sets boundaries, benefits we can all enjoy. The 2019 pandemic altered our working routines significantly, requiring intentional efforts to create predictability, especially amid team disruption. When rethinking routines, involve the team, aligning it with the established vision. Focus on human connection, a crucial element post-pandemic, calming physiology and enhancing resilience. Strive for a balanced weekly routine that facilitates both autonomous work and meaningful team connection. Redesigning routines collaboratively restores predictability, stability, and fosters a sense of togetherness within the team. Empower teams to find solutions collectively, promoting connection, respect for boundaries, and stability.

Enable focus

Flow, a term coined by psychologist Mihaly Csikszentmihalyi, signifies complete immersion in a task, providing a sense of fulfillment. Neural imaging shows reduced activity in busy brain areas related to thinking and more activity in calm focus areas during flow. While team leads cannot create flow experiences, they can encourage them. Focus on three key aspects: clear goals with timely feedback, appropriate challenge levels in tasks, and minimizing distractions to enhance focus. Cultivate a culture that values and supports the pursuit of flow, demonstrating it through your actions and discussions within the team.

Enable flexibility

Navigating the paradox of stability and flexibility as a leader requires honing a skill known as psychological flexibility. Coined by Steven Hayes, it involves tuning into the present moment without judgment and taking action aligned with one's values, even if it means recalculating the route. Encourage your team to engage in frequent check-ins to stay mindful of their emotions and share experiences. Emphasize the importance of staying focused on core values while remaining open to adapting work methods. Establishing non-negotiables, such as team values and goals, can provide a stable foundation amid flexible approaches to work. Developing psychological flexibility is a valuable strategy to support teams in navigating uncertainty effectively.

Foster an experimental mindset

When team members resist change with the phrase "We've always done it that way," it often indicates a reluctance to embrace further change. However, by fostering stability within the team, you can encourage a shift in mindset. Coach your team to view change as an opportunity for improvement, problems as chances to learn, and challenges as experiments. Embracing an entrepreneurial mindset, characterized by risk-taking and continuous learning, empowers the team during periods of change. Cultivate a culture of psychological safety where making mistakes and experimenting are encouraged. Encourage openness to new ideas, but ensure experiments are purposeful and well-researched. Facilitate connections with diverse networks to broaden perspectives and inspire innovative thinking. Despite the discomfort associated with challenging norms, the team can thrive by embracing experimentation.

Build self-efficacy

During the 2020 lockdowns, my family sought distraction through playing an old 1993 Nintendo game, "Super Mario's World". Drawing parallels between the game's chaos and our world, I realized the importance of finding real-life "power ups" to boost capability, confidence, and motivation during uncertainty. Applying Albert Bandura's concept of self-efficacy by three ways to generate stability in your team: identify individual power-ups, foster group power-ups through shared successes, and work on longer-term power-ups for sustained capability enhancement. Boosting self-efficacy through daily successes, both individually and collectively, contributes to resilience in the face of disruption.

Find your power-up

Consider your own needs in leading a team through uncertainty. Leading in challenging times is demanding, and it is crucial to avoid burnout. Reflect on your personal "power up" for today, this week, and the coming months.

Chapter 7 Leading and Motivating People with Different Personalities

What is personality?

As a leader, your role is to guide your team, which is no easy task due to the diverse personalities within it. Understanding the psychology of personality is crucial for effective leadership. Personality, defined by unique patterns of thoughts and behavior, influences how individuals respond to leadership approaches. Recognizing and comprehending the Big Five Personality Traits (openness, conscientiousness, extroversion, agreeableness, neuroticism) on a scale allows you to tailor your leadership, persuasion, and motivation strategies. It is essential to note that these traits are not binary but exist on a spectrum. Obtaining a significant sample size over time is necessary for accurate personality assessments, as moods can fluctuate while traits remain consistent. Before labeling others, start by self-analysis within the Big Five Personality Traits to enhance self-awareness, a crucial aspect of effective leadership.

What motivates people?

When considering motivation, it is not about the temporary excitement often seen on stages but rather the enduring factors that drive individuals, irrespective of their current emotions. Motivation, in this context, refers to the persistent forces steering people's actions. Unlike short-lived hyperemotional states, genuine motivation remains over time, influencing consistent behaviors. Understanding an individual's lasting motivations, akin to the Big Five personality traits, enables the prediction of their actions, enhancing leadership persuasiveness. There are three motivation types: power motivation (desire for influence), affiliation motivation (desire for social connection), and achievement motivation (drive for success and accomplishments).

How personality and motivation can help you lead and manage

Persuasion is akin to a journey, requiring a map to guide you to the destination. Understanding the psychology of personality and motivation provides this roadmap for effective leadership. Persuasion, a vital leadership skill, involves both internal (changing thoughts and feelings) and external (changing behavior) components. Recognizing the diversity in personalities and motivations among team members emphasizes the need for a personalized approach. While one-on-one interactions demand customized messages, group settings may require a more general persuasive approach, considering the commonalities among certain personality types. For those less committed, individual meetings offer the opportunity for tailored discussions based on unique personalities and motivators. In meetings, assess team members' personalities and motivations, allowing for personalized messaging when needed.

Leading extroverts

Understanding extroversion is crucial as it significantly influences how individuals navigate the world. Leading extroverts effectively involves recognizing their need for social interactions to gain energy. Extroverts, talkative and assertive, thrive in roles involving high social interaction, such as business development or sales. Leading extroverts requires obtaining clear commitments, considering their tendency to process externally. It is essential to distinguish between passing thoughts and true commitments, as extroverts may vocalize ideas as a way of processing. To lead extroverts successfully, encourage them to persuade themselves by asking open-ended questions and allowing them to express their thoughts and feelings. Ensure clarity and avoid misconstruing thoughts as commitments in conversations with extroverts.

Leading introverts

To bring out the best in introverts on your team, understand that they derive energy from their inner life. Contrary to a common myth, introverts don't necessarily dislike social interaction but thrive in smaller groups and one-on-one settings. Allow introverts the time they need for internal processing, as they tend to process deeply in silence. Avoid interrupting their thought process prematurely, as vital information may be missed. In communication, recognize that large meetings may not be the most effective for introverts, and opt for more intimate settings before or after meetings to enhance engagement. Acknowledge introverts as valuable team assets due to their thorough processing style and provide them the necessary time and space for contemplation.

Leading ambiverts

Not everyone on your team neatly fits into introvert or extrovert categories; introversion and extroversion exist on a scale. Individuals falling between introvert and extrovert are known as ambiverts or central verts, displaying both introverted and extroverted traits. Recognizing an ambivert in your team requires attention to timing, understanding that social interactions, especially with large groups, may exhaust them. Consider having deep conversations before social events, breaking discussions into smaller, manageable parts, known as micro negotiations. Avoid quick conclusions when assessing personality, remembering it operates on a sliding scale.

Leading highly agreeable people

Leading agreeable people may seem easy, but there are hidden challenges. Agreeable individuals are friendly, polite, and enjoy collaboration. They excel in roles that allow them to be helpful and build connections. However, a key challenge is their tendency to struggle with compliance due to their inclination to avoid conflict by agreeing with others. This people-pleasing behavior can lead to a lack of true commitment to plans. To address this, leaders should recognize the need to invite controlled conflict, prompting agreeable team members to express concerns and objections. Additionally, these individuals may hesitate to contribute in group discussions if their views are unpopular. Leaders must establish psychological safety, building trust to encourage agreeable team members to share their thoughts and contribute meaningfully to discussions.

Leading disagreeable people

Leading disagreeable individuals can be challenging, but it is manageable. Disagreeable people, low in agreeableness, are less concerned about being liked and may express their opinions in an abrasive manner. Recognize that persuading them requires more time, energy, and objective information. Avoid taking it personally and allocate them roles where their strengths can shine, such as in negotiations or playing the devil's advocate in discussions. Acknowledge their critical thinking skills and ensure others understand their role to prevent personal offense. While leading disagreeable individuals may be demanding, understanding and channeling their strengths can make them a valuable asset to the team.

Leading people with varying levels of conscientiousness

Identify the most organized person on your team—likely high in conscientiousness. While reliable and efficient, they may resist change that threatens their reliability. When introducing new programs, address concerns by using targeted open-ended questions that focus on the positive impact of change. For those low in conscientiousness, lacking organization, provide structure without being overly restrictive. Collaborate to create a plan that supports success and gently remind them of agreements when needed. Balancing environments for both high and low conscientiousness promotes optimal performance.

Leading people who are high and low in emotional stability

Addressing emotions in presentations can be challenging due to varying emotional experiences. Neuroticism, a personality trait related to experiencing negative emotions intensely and for extended periods, contributes to emotional differences among individuals. High neuroticism individuals may feel worry, fear, and anxiety more strongly and for a longer duration. Conversely, low neuroticism individuals, like James Bond, appear calm and collected but might lack a sense of urgency. Persuading those high in neuroticism requires addressing their concerns, demonstrating empathy, and involving them in solutions. A listening conversation followed by a discussion that incorporates their fears into proposed solutions can build trust. Patience is crucial when working with high-neuroticism individuals, allowing them time to familiarize themselves with plans and become more comfortable with the situation.

Leading people with varying levels of openness to experience

A friend who frequently shares diverse adventures on social media likely exemplifies high openness to experience—being receptive to new ideas and activities, intellectually curious, and open to experimentation. As a leader, such individuals contribute significantly to brainstorming and ideation, excelling in creative roles. However, the challenge lies in maintaining commitment due to their openness to new experiences. To address this, involve them in the planning process, secure a commitment for a specific duration, and pre-negotiate adjustments through reality testing. On the other hand, individuals low in openness resist change, preferring the status quo. When persuading them, frame adjustments as slight deviations from the current approach, emphasizing familiarity. Understanding your team's openness levels and tailoring your message accordingly is crucial for effective leadership.

Achievement: Motivating competitive people

When considering achievement motivation, it is akin to viewing success as a necessity for survival, as vital as oxygen. As a leader, understanding and mobilizing this ambition can enhance team and company performance. Achievement motivation is a desire to perform at a high level, acquire new skills, and experience perceived wins. Identifying individuals with this motivation involves listening to their stories, focusing on keywords like win, lose, earn, and gain, and observing their office for awards and achievements. To maximize their potential, frame messages in terms of personal improvement or wins, aligning with their identified motivations. However, be aware that individuals high in achievement motivation may shy away from tasks with a high likelihood of failure, preferring challenges where success is attainable. Despite potential downsides, leveraging their competitive energy and providing winnable opportunities can make them valuable assets to your team.

Power: Motivating those who seek influence

Leading someone motivated by power requires understanding their desire for influence rather than necessarily authoritarian control. Individuals with power motivation seek to improve their status and impact others. Recognizing them in your team involves identifying those who join groups to enhance their roles or stifle discussions. They tend to be persuasive, potentially overshadowing diverse ideas. As a leader, ensure an inclusive decision-making process, limiting their dominance creatively. Address their desire for advancement by highlighting how high performance in their current role positions them for progression within the organization. To effectively lead them, align their aspirations for prestige, status, and influence with the goals of your organization.

Affiliation: Motivating socially oriented people

Leading someone high in affiliation motivation involves recognizing their strong desire for social interaction. Unlike introversion or extroversion, this motivation is about the enjoyment and happiness derived from connecting with others. It is crucial to understand that these individuals may struggle to perform without sufficient interaction. Placing them in roles that foster collaboration and allow for interaction is essential to maintaining their morale and maximizing their contributions.

Promotion vs. prevention focus

Tailoring your message based on whether your team member is prevention-focused or promotion-focused can significantly enhance the persuasiveness of your communication. Prevention-focused individuals are risk-averse, prioritizing safety and protection, so frame your message in terms of security. Understand their concerns, and address them directly, emphasizing how your proposal mitigates risks. On the other hand, promotion-focused individuals are motivated by gains and achievements. Focus on what they stand to gain, aligning your message with their goals. Ask questions to uncover their objectives and frame your proposal as a pathway to their desired accomplishments. Whether emphasizing risk or reward, adapting your message to your team member's focus enhances the effectiveness of your persuasion.

Create new and better results with your team

You've gained valuable strategies to enhance your leadership skills by understanding the psychology of personality and motivation. Now, apply this knowledge to connect, persuade, understand, and empathize more effectively with your team. Take these insights beyond theory and apply them in real-life leadership, negotiation, and conflict resolution situations.

Chapter 8 Human Leadership

Communicate often to improve employee experience

Amid the 2019 pandemic, global communications company, Edelman discovered that 63% of employees sought daily updates from leaders, with 20% desiring communication multiple times a day. Despite concerns about repetition, consistent communication is now more crucial than ever. Chipotle's CEO, Brian Niccol, emphasized the increased frequency of communication during the pandemic, noting monthly meetings instead of biannual ones. This shift allowed for greater agility and adaptability in response to rapid changes. CEOs, including Niccol, recognize the strategic value of communication, and it is crucial for leaders to adopt a thoughtful communication strategy, regardless of the circumstances. Reflect on your communication frequency and consider developing a deliberate communication plan. Your team likely values more communication than you might realize.

Find the sweet spot between tech and connect

Ever wonder why video meetings are the default, leading to high fatigue? Stanford researcher Jeremy Bailenson calls it "nonverbal overload." To be effective communicators, we must find a sweet spot between technology and connection. Bill Koenigsberg, CEO of Horizon Media, exemplifies this well. During the pandemic, he diversified communication mediums—town hall meetings, daily emails, and video calls for work anniversaries. This variety fosters connection, positively impacting both employees and business outcomes. Consider mixing up communication mediums and conducting a communication audit to find your sweet spot between tech and connect.

Be vulnerable as a leader

Vulnerability and authenticity, often considered buzzwords, are about honesty in communication. Employees value leaders who are real and human. Harvard Business Review notes that when leaders communicate authentically and vulnerably, employees feel hope and trust, improving performance. Avner Mendelson, former CEO of Bank Leumi USA, exemplifies this. His weekly emails during the pandemic, sharing personal struggles and joys, increased employee engagement. Reflect on past experiences of adding more of yourself in communication. Consider incorporating honesty gradually, fostering connections and positive impact.

Have a clear meeting purpose

Meetings have become abundant, with data showing a significant increase since the pandemic. To ensure effective meetings, a clear and specific purpose is crucial. Priya Parker, in "The Art of Gathering," highlights that focused gatherings generate more passion. Specific purposes also help limit attendance to those contributing to the topic, reducing the overall number of meetings. Examples include Intel's requirement for meetings to inform, discuss, or decide on specific topics. A purpose audit, evaluating the purpose of each meeting, can lead to a substantial reduction in unnecessary meetings, optimizing time use.

Be present and engaged in meetings

Presence in virtual meetings is more crucial than ever, challenging leaders as attendees often turn off video and succumb to multitasking. Recognizing the importance of true presence is the initial step. While video fatigue is real, some leaders, like the one from Herman Miller, request cameras on for a weekly meeting to emphasize the human connection. Eileen Fisher sets the tone with a chime for a moment of quiet, fostering presence. Microsoft CEO Satya Nadella engages leaders with "Researcher of the Amazing," sharing impactful stories to captivate attention. Leaders should employ strategies to keep attendees focused, aligning with the company culture for a simple yet personal touch.

Road tested tips for meetings

Most people would prefer a dentist visit over a bad meeting, and they often blame managers for the meeting overload. IBM's CEO created a pledge to address this issue, focusing on setting boundaries, preventing video fatigue, and optimizing meeting durations. Effective protocols for managing hybrid meetings include one person, one screen, ending the meeting when remote employees leave, and incorporating personal connections at the start. Tailor your protocols to your business needs, industry, company values, and management style to ensure more productive meetings.

Retain employees by offering them ways to grow

Record numbers of people are leaving their jobs, and research from Deloitte highlights that offering professional development is a highly effective retention strategy. ExecuSearch's report further reveals that 86% of professionals would consider changing jobs for more development opportunities. Companies like Betterment provide one-on-one coaching, with directors and above receiving six sessions per year and others receiving three. TruckStop.com incorporates professional development into onboarding, using the Myers-Briggs assessment to help employees create plans for their best work. Prioritizing personal and professional development from the start can significantly impact employee engagement and retention. Make professional development a central focus to address retention challenges effectively.

Use the 80/20 rule to spark curiosity

Consider the renowned 20% case study at Google, where employees are encouraged to spend 20% of their time on personal innovation alongside core projects. Google's data-driven approach supports the notion that allowing employees to explore their curiosity for even 20% of their time results in individual and business flourishing. Harvard Business Review findings emphasize the advantages of cultivating curiosity in employees, including enhanced creativity, innovation, communication, team performance, decision-making, and reduced group conflict. Embrace and implement opportunities for employees to follow their curiosity, recognizing that it contributes positively to both individuals and business outcomes.

Support professional development during work hours

While it may seem challenging to balance day-to-day tasks with employee development, incorporating learning into the workday can yield significant benefits. A Salesforce report reveals that 59% of the US workforce has experienced reduced learning opportunities since March 2020. However, when organizations invest more in learning and development, a Salesforce survey indicates that 74% of respondents would be more productive, 72% more engaged, and 69% happier with their work. EA Markets, a virtual financial services firm, successfully incorporates professional development into its monthly in-person meetings, fostering growth through activities like lunch-and-learns and senior leader interviews. Evaluate existing professional development programs in your organization, consider their integration into the workday, and explore new opportunities for growth. Whether it is an hour, a week, a day, or a month, scheduling professional development now can lead to positive outcomes.

Walk the walk as a leader

Amidst the heightened awareness of stress and wellbeing, addressing mental health challenges is crucial, especially with the increasing overlap of work and personal life, particularly for remote workers. An analogy drawn from airplane safety underscores the point: just as you are instructed to secure your oxygen mask before assisting others, prioritizing your own wellbeing sets a foundation for a healthier workplace. The bottom line is impacted when organizations lack a wellbeing culture; a 2021 Gallup survey links employee struggles with twice the turnover rate. To lead by example, openly discuss your challenges, embrace a work-life balance by attending personal commitments proudly, and consistently emphasize the importance of both physical and mental wellness. Despite 70% of CEOs claiming acceptance of mental health issues, only 35% of employees believe this to be true. The pandemic has elevated the significance of creating a culture of wellness, urging human leaders to take concrete steps, beginning with self-care and transparent communication to set the tone for the entire organization.

Check in with your people a lot

Returning to normalcy is a natural desire, but in the realm of workplace well-being, life remains anything but normal. Initially, leaders dedicated substantial time to checking in with employees during the pandemic, but as we approach regular business operations, finding the balance between check-ins and productivity has become a leadership challenge. However, consistent and brief check-ins are crucial for both employee well-being and organizational success. Research indicates that regular check-ins make employees feel supported and lead to fewer mental health challenges. Unfortunately, only 39% of employees feel supported by their managers, emphasizing the need for more attention to well-being. Simple and genuine check-ins, such as asking employees how they're truly doing, contribute significantly to building a culture of wellness. Examples include Dropbox's approach of asking, "How are you really, really doing?" and another company's practice of sharing one word describing their feelings at the start of each meeting. Despite initial concerns about repetition, studies show that employees appreciate and even request daily updates, highlighting the positive impact of regular check-ins on building a wellness-oriented organizational culture.

One size does not fit all for well-being

Recognizing the impact of employee well-being on job retention, leaders face added pressure to address these challenges. The positive aspect is that there's no universal approach to instilling a well-being culture in organizations, allowing leaders to tailor solutions based on their company values. Examples include Meetup, where CEO David Siegel redirected office space funds to provide individualized wellness stipends for employees. National Business Capital incorporates morning stretches at 9:01 a.m. daily, contributing to a positive start and acting as a mini meditation. Citigroup's CEO Jane Fraser introduced Zoom-Free Fridays to address the toll of blurred lines between home and work during the relentless pandemic workday. Building a wellness culture involves closely aligning with employee needs and organizational values, avoiding a one-size-fits-all approach.

Practice human leadership

To enhance your human leadership skills, embrace intentionality. The four key elements include: 1) fostering connections through communication, 2) reconsidering meeting structures, 3) acknowledging that professional development concerns everyone, and 4) cultivating a culture of wellbeing. Keep in mind that human leadership is not one-size-fits-all; tailor it to your company and self. Although it involves hard work, the benefits are substantial. Remember being a human leader is beneficial for individuals, excellent for business, and has the potential to make a positive impact on the world.

Chapter 9 Talking About Mental Health as a Leader

Apply what works for your specific leadership journey

While a one-size-fits-all solution on discussing mental health at work may seem reassuring, it is important to acknowledge that such certainty does not exist. Beware of anyone claiming otherwise, as it may be a marketing tactic or an attempt to appear as an all-knowing expert. No one possesses that level of expertise. Approach the shared content critically, adapt it to your unique role, team dynamics, and company culture. Successful implementation hinges on tailoring the information to your specific circumstances. As a leader, remember that you, too, are an individual with mental health considerations. Regardless of your role, addressing your mental health needs is valid. If discussing your mental health with your manager seems challenging due to leadership expectations, This book serves as an educational and informational purposes only and does not substitute professional advice in psychological, medical, legal, HR, or other areas. Seek appropriate care or guidance for mental health issues beyond the scope of workplace conversations.

Important definitions

Precise terminology is crucial when discussing mental health at work. Mental health refers to your baseline social, emotional, and cognitive functioning, encompassing a broad spectrum of emotions. Stress, often perceived negatively, is a neutral concept indicating a need for adjustment or response, with both positive and negative forms. Mental illness denotes behavioral health conditions affecting emotions, behavior, or thinking, with over 300 types ranging from mild to severe. One in four people, pre-pandemic, experienced mental illness in their lifetime, and it's on a concerning upward trend. Mental illness can result from various factors, and individuals do not choose to have it. People with mental illness are often high-functioning, leading typical lives while managing their condition. Key takeaways: accurate definitions foster informed discussions at work, and many silently grapple with mental illness, emphasizing the need for understanding and support.

Shifting how we understand, approach, and lead

Avoiding discussions about mental health at work is no longer an option. Such avoidance, once encouraged or feared for legal reasons, is outdated. While some mental health conversations may be complex, many are straightforward. Reflect on personal experiences and team dynamics when facing challenges. The traditional work-life partition has eroded, acknowledging the unrealistic nature of separating personal and professional spheres. Despite potential complications, leaders must engage in these conversations, considering their responsibility for team productivity, development, and well-being. Leaders are not expected to become therapists but should recognize the importance of cultivating trust through acknowledging and addressing mental health concerns. The goal is to develop mental health conversations as a core leadership skill, emphasizing boundaries and responsibilities.

Conversational literacy for core leadership development

Leaders are trained in various skills, from safety protocols to performance reviews, highlighting the importance of applying such knowledge. However, the skill of discussing mental health at work is often treated differently. As a people leader, ongoing training in effective management, building psychological safety, and addressing mental health is essential. Despite organizational approaches, leaders should recognize this skill's significance and take personal responsibility for its development. While the world of work has managers who neglect this aspect, investing in learning how to discuss mental health constructively is crucial. Key takeaways include acknowledging mental health discussions as a vital leadership skill, taking personal responsibility for skill development, and recognizing the importance of providing this skillset to one's team. If team members are hesitant to discuss mental health, understanding conversational obstacles is crucial for managers.

Understanding mental health conversation obstacles

While society has long promoted education on mental health, many individuals remain fearful of discussing it. The conditioning to avoid such conversations stems from various influences, including family, gender identity, culture, social circles, religion, media, and past negative experiences. Even within the workplace, discussing mental health with a manager can evoke anxiety for both leaders and employees. The professional world historically deemed personal matters inappropriate for work, fostering a culture of avoidance. Today, workplace cultures, emotionally stoic leaders, and inappropriate jokes contribute to this stigma. Despite societal progress, discussing mental health remains deeply personal, impacting whether employees feel comfortable opening up, especially to influential figures like their leaders. As a leader, it is essential to consider your team members' experiences beyond the professional relationship, understand their fears, and be aware of potential contributions to their apprehension. Recognizing these obstacles is the first step toward fostering a more open environment for mental health discussions.

Humanizing yourself as a leader through role modeling

Encouraging someone to share their struggles is often easier than admitting one's own challenges, especially in a manager-direct-report relationship where power dynamics traditionally favor one-way support. However, the shift away from leadership stoicism is positive for two reasons. First, leaders discussing mental health humanize themselves and demonstrate openness. Second, such transparency sets an example for team members, making it more likely for them to open up. Acknowledging your own mental health challenges as a leader is essential. Reflecting on your well-being, sharing truthfully, and demonstrating a commitment to managing challenges can strengthen team dynamics. Key takeaways: 1) Role modeling mental health discussions helps create an open environment. 2) Prioritizing your mental health is crucial for effective leadership. 3) Talking about mental health demonstrates self-awareness and responsibility, not weakness.

Understanding your responsibilities and setting boundaries

As a manager, it is crucial to recognize that you are not obligated to solve your team members' problems or alleviate their discomfort. You are not their therapist, parent, or family member. Reflect on why you want to discuss their mental health and set clear boundaries. Your responsibilities do not include providing ongoing informal counseling or sheltering them from typical job-related stress. It is your responsibility to show authentic care, be aware of how mental health struggles may affect work, encourage openness, and, in emergency situations, involve HR or health professionals. Support your team within the boundaries of your role, emphasizing their responsibility in addressing and managing their struggles.

Understanding why triaging matters

When discussing mental health with your team, it is essential to establish boundaries and practice triaging. Triage involves assessing the situation, determining your ability to help, and redirecting team members to appropriate resources when necessary. Acknowledge that you may not be the best person to assist with certain issues, just as a specialist in one area may not be an expert in others. If a team member requires help beyond your expertise, express empathy, and guide them toward the relevant person or professional. Ensure they understand that your priority is their well-being and that seeking specialized help is in their best interest. Offer assistance in connecting with resources, but respect their decision if they prefer to handle it independently.

Starting the conversation

If you are considering discussing a team member's mental health, it is commendable and shows your supportive leadership. However, it is crucial to understand that they are not obligated to share, and your approach matters. Avoid assuming the cause of their struggles and focus on providing support without implying assumptions. Consider three logistical pointers: 1) Avoid evaluative discussions like annual reviews, 2) Choose appropriate communication channels (avoid written channels for initial concerns), and 3) Be mindful of the time and place. Clearly state your intention behind the conversation and express care and concern. When initiating the conversation, share your objective observations rather than using clinical language. For example, say, "I've noticed changes, and you seem unhappy. Is everything okay? I'm here if you want to talk." If the team member is willing to engage, use in-the-moment techniques during the conversation.

In the moment techniques

In the conversation, focus on asking thoughtful questions, such as inquiring about the type of help your team member desires and using open-ended questions to understand the situation better. Towards the end, ask action-oriented questions to assess their next steps. Respond by being fully present, actively listening, and avoiding generic platitudes. Refrain from giving advice unless they express openness to your experience. Prioritize confidentiality unless it is an emergency. In the case of disclosures about mental health, consult HR for legal implications. When navigating next steps, collaborate if you can work together or guide them to appropriate resources using the triaging concept.

Receiving the conversation

When a team member initiates a conversation about their mental health, your response is crucial. Emphasizing the importance of this moment, it is an opportunity to commend their courage and express appreciation for their openness. Ensure they feel valued for reaching out. If you are unable to engage at the moment due to a deadline or personal state, be honest about it and suggest rescheduling. Avoid faking support or transferring stress. When resuming the conversation, use triaging skills to assess your ability to help and apply effective communication strategies. If the conversation does not go smoothly or a team member consistently struggles emotionally without opening up, challenging scenarios may arise.

Unexpected misunderstandings or an unwillingness to talk

When misunderstandings arise in these conversations, approach it by acknowledging the perceived misunderstanding. Avoid telling them what they feel; instead, share your observation, clarify your intention, and express your willingness to understand better. If they decline to elaborate, respect their choice and express your readiness to continue the conversation at a later time.

If a direct report seeks assistance beyond your capability, such as worsening mental health affecting work, delicately explain your observation, offer insights, and establish a boundary. Address situations where a team member consistently neglects mental health, impacting performance. Collaborate with HR for guidance, emphasizing accountability without singling them out for mental health issues. If resistance persists, HR intervention may be necessary, acknowledging the complexity of such scenarios. While outcomes are uncertain, responding responsibly, empathetically, and professionally is crucial as a leader.

Building on your mental health leadership skills

We've covered a range of topics, addressing the purpose of conversations with your team, overcoming discussion obstacles, navigating the conversation process, and managing challenging moments. As you conclude, consider how you will apply this knowledge. Recognize that becoming an expert overnight is unrealistic and unnecessary. Skill development requires intentional, gradual efforts. Commit to ongoing leadership development by asking yourself: Why am I motivated to do this? When and how will I start practicing? What aspects do I need improvement on? How will I evaluate my progress? Who can provide feedback on my improvement? Regularly revisit these questions to adapt and refine your approach.